HAIKU BIBLE

PIRA TRITASAVIT

JOIN THE COMMUNITY

https://www.facebook.com/groups/HaikuBible/

WRITE YOUR OWN

http://bit.ly/HaikuBible

Be not rash with your mouth, nor let your heart
be hasty to utter a word before God,
for God is in heaven and you are on earth.
Therefore let your words be few.

ECCLESIASTES 5:2

THE OLD TESTAMENT

Torah / Pentateuch
History of Israel
Wisdom & Poetry
Major Prophets
Minor Prophets

THE NEW TESTAMENT

Gospels of Jesus & Acts
Paul's Letters
Others' Letters
Revelation

THE OLD TESTAMENT

TORAH / PENTATEUCH

GENESIS

Creation, all good
Mankind rebels, God pursues
God makes good from bad

EXODUS

Red Sea Salvation
Manna, quail, commandments, calf
Show me Your glory!

LEVITICUS

Bloody atonement
The LORD alone is holy
Worship must be pure

NUMBERS

Bronze serpent: Look! Live!
The LORD bless you and keep you
God speaks through an ass

DEUTERONOMY

Hear: the LORD is one
Love God with all your heart, soul
Obey and be blessed

HISTORY OF ISRAEL

JOSHUA

Be strong, courageous
Worship IS warfare! Walls fall!
Choose whom you will serve

JUDGES

Disobedience
No kings to rule; judges raised
Right in their own eyes

RUTH

Loyalty through loss
Widow redeemed by kinsman
Line of King David

1 SAMUEL

"We demand a king!"
Saul anointed, then David
God looks at the heart

2 SAMUEL

How the mighty fall!
Glory, scandal, cover-up
And God sees it all

1 KINGS

King Solomon's reign
Wisdom, temple, wayward wives
Kings fail; prophets raised

2 KINGS

Most kings are evil
Prophets proclaim God's anger
Remnant will be saved

1 CHRONICLES

Genealogies
Deeds of Kings: Saul and David
Then Solomon's start

2 CHRONICLES

Fall of the kingdoms
Sin, evil, idolatry
Jerusalem burned

EZRA

Rebuild wall, God's house
Teach, do the law of the LORD
People confess sin

NEHEMIAH

Rebuild God's people
Strap on a sword; keep building
Wall dedicated

ESTHER

King's beauty pageant
God raised a Queen to save Jews
Celebrate Purim

Wisdom & Poetry

JOB

God gives, takes away
Why? Wrong opinions abound
God restores, and more

PSALMS

Sing hallelujah!
His love endures forever
Let all that breathe praise

PROVERBS

The fear of the LORD
Trust in the LORD, acknowledge
Walk with the wise, grow

ECCLESIASTES

Time for everything
All meaningless...but fear God
Let your words be few

SONG OF SONGS

Holy, sexy love
His banner over me: love
Love's as strong as death

Major Prophets

ISAIAH

Prince of Peace foretold
Stricken—by His wounds, we're healed
Our deeds, filthy rags

JEREMIAH

Return, faithless ones
I know the plans: future, hope
New covenant hearts

LAMENTATIONS

The LORD's steadfast love:
UNENDING! Mercies renewed
Your faithfulness: GREAT!

EZEKIEL

Heart of stone, of flesh
Adopted, adorned, atoned
Prophesy, "Bones, live!"

DANIEL

Kingdoms felled by stone
God rescues from flames and den
Writing on the wall

MINOR PROPHETS

HOSEA

God: "Marry that whore!"
Hosea obeys...and loves
The point? God's great grace!

JOEL

Rend hearts, not garments
Restore years lost to locusts
Spirit will pour out

AMOS

Seek the LORD and live
Let justice roll like waters
Righteousness like streams

OBADIAH

Don't gloat over bros
The day of the LORD is near
Kingdom shall be His

JONAH

Prophet flees from God
Resents God's mercy on all
Why shouldn't God save?

MICAH

Beat swords to plowshares
All shall sit, vine and fig tree
What does God require?

NAHUM

Jealous Avenger
Down with evil Nineveh!
LORD restores Jacob

HABAKKUK

Righteous live by faith
In wrath, remember mercy
Though no fruit, rejoice!

ZEPHANIAH

I'll change them, pure speech
I'll exult o'er you with song
Change shame into praise

HAGGAI

LORD's house in ruins
Paneled homes, hole-bag wages
Latter-house glory

ZECHARIAH

All flesh be silent
Not by might, nor by power
But by my spirit

MALACHI

"How has God loved us?"
Don't rob God; test Him with tithes
Turn dads' and sons' hearts

THE NEW TESTAMENT

GOSPELS OF JESUS & ACTS

MATTHEW

Sermon on the mount
Love the Lord...AND your neighbor
Go make disciples

MARK

"Immediately"
Shortest Gospel of Jesus
Does Mark flee naked?

LUKE

Twelve year old Jesus
Lost sheep, lost coin, two lost sons
Wowed in Emmaus!

JOHN

God so loved the world
Believe: Resurrection, life!
That they may be one

ACTS

Holy Spirit fills
Disciples spread, preach, heal, die
Who woulda thunk Paul?

PAUL'S LETTERS

ROMANS

Sin–death; free gift–life!
No condemnation in Christ
Living sacrifice

1 CORINTHIANS

Cross: power of God
Faith, hope, love—greatest is love
Death, where is your sting?

2 CORINTHIANS

Christ became our sin
We became God's righteousness
Grace is sufficient

GALATIANS

Freedom, not foreskin
Live by fruit of the Spirit
Boast in cross of Christ

EPHESIANS

By grace, saved through faith
Can't comprehend God's great love
Put on God's armor

PHILIPPIANS

To live, Christ; die, gain!
Imitate the humble Christ
Do all through Christ's strength

COLOSSIANS

Jesus, God's fullness
Christ in you, hope of glory
Debt nailed to the cross

1 THESSALONIANS

Not man's word; God's word
The Lord will come like a thief
Rejoice, pray, give thanks

2 THESSALONIANS

Let none deceive you
God called you; therefore, stand firm
Beware idleness

1 TIMOTHY

Trust these words: Christ saves
Pray for all; noble leaders
Godly contentment

2 TIMOTHY

Rightly handle truth
All Scripture is breathed by God
Beware itching ears

TITUS

To the pure, all's pure
Grace of God appeared for all
Once fools, now we're heirs

PHILEMON

From slave to brother
Once "useless", now he's "useful"
Obey and do more

OTHERS' LETTERS

HEBREWS

Jesus is supreme
God swears by God...none greater
Live AND die BY FAITH

JAMES

Faith sans works is dead
The tongue is hell's forest fire
Life is a mist...poof!

1 PETER

Living hope is born
Living stones on Cornerstone
Follow in His steps

2 PETER

Confirm your calling
Scripture from Holy Spirit
One day, thousand years

1 JOHN

God is light; be cleansed
Antichrist denies God's son
Love one another

2 JOHN

Truth abides in us
Love: Walk in His commandments
Watch for deceivers

3 JOHN

Joy! Kids walk in truth
Imitate good, not evil
You know that we're true

JUDE

Contend for the faith
Be alert, grumblers, stumblers
Now to Him--GLORY!

REVELATION

REVELATION

Alpha, Omega
Lamb who was slain, He's worthy!
Christ, come soon! Amen.

JOIN THE COMMUNITY

WRITE YOUR OWN

NOTES

NOTES

NOTES

NOTES

NOTES

NOTES

NOTES

NOTES

NOTES

NOTES

NOTES

NOTES

NOTES

NOTES

NOTES

Contact the author
pira@kingdompros.com
Love to hear from you =)

Stay tuned for the forthcoming
Audiobook MP3 version
of Haiku Bible